CHAMC[illegible]
MONT-BI[illegible]
TRAVEL GUIDE

PAMELA COUTLER

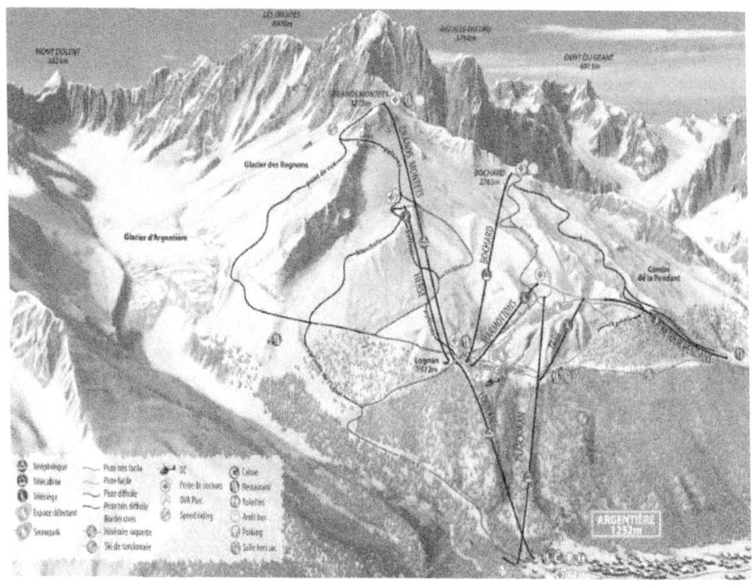
DENT DU GEANT
Glacier des Rognons
Glacier d'Argentière
BOCHARD
Combe de la Pendant
MARMOTTONS
Lognan
ARGENTIÈRE

TABLE OF CONTENT

TRAVEL PLANNER

TRAVEL PLANNER

DESTINATION:

DATES:

MON	TUES	WED	THURS	FRI	SAT	SUN

SIGHTS TO SEE:

PLACES TO EAT:

EXCURSIONS:

FLIGHT DETAILS:

PAMELA COUTLER

TRAVEL PLANNER

TRAVEL PLANNER

DESTINATION:

DATES:

MON	TUES	WED	THURS	FRI	SAT	SUN

SIGHTS TO SEE: ---------------------- ---------------------- ---------------------- ---------------------- ----------------------

PLACES TO EAT: ---------------------- ---------------------- ---------------------- ---------------------- ----------------------

EXCURSIONS: ---------------------- ---------------------- ---------------------- ---------------------- ----------------------

FLIGHT DETAILS:

PAMELA COUTLER

CHAPTER ONE:

INTRODUCTION TO CHAMONIX MONT-BLANC

Overview of Chamonix Mont-Blanc

Nestled within the pristine embrace of the French Alps, Chamonix Mont-Blanc stands as a quintessential alpine jewel, captivating visitors with its unparalleled beauty and diverse offerings. At the heart of the Haute-Savoie region, Chamonix is renowned as the "Gateway to the European Cascades" and is dominated by the majestic Mont-Blanc, Western Europe's highest peak.

The town itself is a harmonious blend of tradition and modernity, with cobblestone streets winding through a picturesque landscape of chalet-style architecture. Chamonix's rich history as a mountaineering hub is evident in its charming town squares and historical landmarks. Visitors can explore sites like the Church of Saint-Michel, dating back to the 18th century, and the Alpine Museum, which chronicles the region's mountaineering heritage.

The real allure of Chamonix lies in its natural wonders. The Mont-Blanc massif, with its towering peaks and glaciers, serves as a playground for outdoor enthusiasts. Whether you're an avid hiker, a passionate skier, or a thrill-seeker, Chamonix offers a plethora of activities against a backdrop of breathtaking vistas. The Aiguille du Midi cable car provides a panoramic ascent to dizzying heights, affording unparalleled views of the Alps.

Chamonix is not merely a destination for adrenaline junkies; it's also a haven for those seeking tranquility. The town boasts a vibrant cultural scene, with art galleries, boutique shops, and a welcoming atmosphere in its local establishments. Culinary delights await at every turn, as Chamonix offers a delectable array of Savoyard cuisine, best enjoyed in cozy mountain-side eateries.

With a climate that varies from snowy winters to pleasant summers, Chamonix beckons visitors year-round. The guide will delve into the intricacies of the town, unveiling its secrets and guiding travelers through an unforgettable exploration of Chamonix Mont-Blanc, where nature's grandeur meets cultural charm.

Historical Significance

Chamonix Mont-Blanc's historical tapestry is woven with tales of exploration, adventure, and pioneering spirit, making it a place of immense historical significance. The roots of Chamonix's importance trace back to the 18th century when the town emerged as a vital hub for Alpine tourism and mountaineering.

The turning point in Chamonix's history occurred in 1741 when two Englishmen, William Windham and Richard Pococke, explored the region. Their writings sparked interest in the Alps as a destination for the burgeoning Romantic movement, drawing artists, writers, and scientists to the area. Chamonix quickly became a focal point for intellectual and artistic endeavors, its dramatic landscapes serving as inspiration for poets like Lord Byron and Percy Bysshe Shelley.

In the 19th century, Chamonix solidified its reputation as a mountaineering center, attracting renowned climbers like Jacques Balmat and Michel-Gabriel Paccard, who completed the first successful ascent of Mont-Blanc in 1786. This achievement marked the birth of modern mountaineering and established Chamonix as the de facto base for those seeking to conquer the Alps.

The town's development continued with the advent of the Golden Age of Alpinism in the mid-19th century. Chamonix became a haven for alpinists from across Europe, with the establishment of the Compagnie des Guides in 1821, making it the oldest mountain guiding company in the world. This institution played a pivotal role in shaping Chamonix's identity as a center for alpine exploration.

The early 20th century saw Chamonix hosting the first Winter Olympics in 1924, solidifying its status as a premier destination for winter sports. The influx of tourists, coupled with ongoing advancements in transportation infrastructure, further propelled the town's growth and international appeal.

Today, Chamonix stands as a living testament to its rich history, with historic structures like the Church of Saint-Michel and the Maison de la Montagne serving as reminders of its past. The town's streets, once trodden by early mountaineers, exude an air of nostalgia, inviting modern-day visitors to step back in time and appreciate the historical significance that has shaped Chamonix Mont-Blanc into the iconic destination it is today.

Geographical Features

Chamonix Mont-Blanc, nestled in the Rhône-Alpes region of southeastern France, boasts a diverse and awe-inspiring landscape shaped by the majestic peaks of the Mont-Blanc massif. The geographical features of this region contribute to its allure as a year-round destination for outdoor enthusiasts.

Mont-Blanc Massif:

At the heart of Chamonix lies the iconic Mont-Blanc massif, a snow-capped mountain range that includes Mont-Blanc, Western Europe's highest peak standing at 4,810 meters (15,781 feet).

This massif encompasses several other notable summits, including Aiguille du Midi, Aiguille Verte, and the Dôme du Goûter. Glaciers, such as the Mer de Glace, further characterize the rugged beauty of the massif.

Valleys and Gorges:

Chamonix is situated in the Chamonix Valley, carved by glacial erosion over centuries. This U-shaped valley is flanked by towering peaks on either side, creating a dramatic and picturesque setting.

The river Arve flows through the valley, contributing to the formation of deep gorges and valleys, providing stunning vistas at every turn.

Lakes and Waterfalls:

The region is adorned with pristine alpine lakes and cascading waterfalls. Lake Blanc, Lac Cornu, and Lac de Cheserys are just a few examples of the glacial lakes dotting the landscape.

Waterfalls, such as the impressive Cascade du Dard, add to the enchanting scenery, creating natural wonders that are accessible through hiking trails.

Alpine Meadows and Flora:

Chamonix is not just about towering peaks; it also features alpine meadows adorned with a colorful array of wildflowers.

In the warmer months, these meadows burst into bloom, creating a vibrant contrast to the snow-clad peaks.

The diverse flora includes edelweiss, gentians, and alpine roses, adding a touch of botanical beauty to the landscape.

Rock Formations and Caves:

The region is characterized by rugged rock formations, including limestone and granite, sculpted by the forces of nature. Cave systems, such as the Grotte de Glace (Ice Cave), offer unique opportunities for exploration.

The juxtaposition of rock and ice creates a mesmerizing geological tapestry.

Chamonix Mont-Blanc's geographical features provide a playground for a myriad of outdoor activities, from skiing down snow-covered slopes in winter to hiking through alpine meadows in summer. The varied terrain ensures that every corner of this picturesque destination is a testament to the Earth's natural wonders, inviting visitors to immerse themselves in the beauty and grandeur of the French Alps.

Climate and Best Times to Visit

Chamonix Mont-Blanc experiences a classic Alpine climate, characterized by distinct seasons that offer varied experiences for visitors. Understanding the climate is crucial for planning activities, as each season brings its own charm and opportunities.

Winter (December to February):

Winter transforms Chamonix into a snowy wonderland, attracting skiers and snowboarders from around the globe. The winter months, December through February, see temperatures ranging from -2°C to 7°C (28°F to 45°F) in the valley, while the higher elevations experience colder conditions. The town is adorned with a blanket of snow, and the ski resorts, such as Chamonix-Mont-Blanc and Argentière, come alive. Winter sports enthusiasts can revel in pristine slopes, and the Aiguille du Midi cable car provides access to breathtaking panoramic views of the snow-covered peaks.

Spring (March to May):

Spring in Chamonix is a time of transition, with melting snow giving way to blooming alpine meadows. March sees lingering winter conditions, but as temperatures rise, April and May bring milder weather, with temperatures ranging from 3°C to 15°C (37°F to 59°F). This season is ideal for those seeking a mix of winter sports and the beauty of emerging spring landscapes. Hiking trails become accessible, and cascading waterfalls are at their peak, creating a picturesque backdrop.

Summer (June to August):

Summer is a delightful season in Chamonix, with temperatures ranging from 8°C to 23°C (46°F to 73°F). The snow retreats, revealing verdant landscapes, and alpine flora blooms. Summer is perfect for hiking, rock climbing, and exploring the extensive network of trails. The longer days provide ample sunlight for adventure activities, and outdoor enthusiasts can engage in mountain biking, paragliding, and relaxing by the serene alpine lakes.

Autumn (September to November):

Autumn paints Chamonix with a palette of warm hues as the foliage changes colors. September still offers pleasant weather, with temperatures ranging from 6°C to 18°C (43°F to 64°F). It's an excellent time for hiking, and as the season progresses, the town experiences quieter periods. By November, the first snowfall graces the peaks, setting the stage for the upcoming winter season.

The best times to visit Chamonix depend on individual preferences and interests. Winter is ideal for snow sports enthusiasts, while summer attracts hikers and outdoor adventurers. Spring and autumn offer a balance between the two, providing a mix of activities and a chance to witness the changing landscapes. Understanding Chamonix's climate allows visitors to tailor their experience and make the most of this enchanting Alpine destination throughout the year.

Getting There: Transportation Options

Chamonix Mont-Blanc, nestled in the French Alps, is well-connected, offering a range of transportation options to suit various preferences and travel styles. Whether arriving from nearby cities or international locations, the town provides efficient and picturesque ways to access its breathtaking landscapes.

1. **By Air:**

The closest major airport to Chamonix is Geneva Airport (GVA) in Switzerland, approximately 88 kilometers (55 miles) away. Travelers can opt for direct flights to Geneva from major cities worldwide. From the airport, various transportation options, including shuttle services, private transfers, and rental cars, are available to reach Chamonix. Other airports within a reasonable distance include Lyon-Saint Exupéry Airport and Milan Malpensa Airport.

2. **By Train:**

Chamonix has a well-connected railway station, making train travel a scenic and convenient option. The French SNCF network provides direct services to Chamonix from major cities like Paris, Lyon, and Geneva. The Mont-Blanc Express, a charming narrow-gauge railway, connects Chamonix to Martigny in Switzerland, offering breathtaking views along the way.

3. By Car:

Driving to Chamonix allows flexibility and the opportunity to explore the surrounding regions. The town is accessible by road through the A40 motorway from Geneva or the A41 from Annecy. The journey offers stunning views of the Alps, and rental car services are available at major airports and cities. Keep in mind that winter conditions may require snow chains and careful navigation.

4. By Bus and Shuttle Services:

Several bus and shuttle services operate between Chamonix and neighboring towns, airports, and ski resorts. These services provide a cost-effective and environmentally friendly option for travelers. The Chamonix Valley also offers a free bus service, facilitating easy movement within the town and surrounding areas.

5. By Helicopter:

For a truly exclusive and scenic arrival, helicopter services are available from Geneva Airport to Chamonix. This luxurious mode of transportation not only reduces travel time but also provides a bird's-eye view of the stunning Alpine landscape.

6. Local Transportation:

Once in Chamonix, the town is easily navigable on foot, and its compact size allows visitors to explore its attractions at a leisurely pace.

Additionally, cable cars, cogwheel trains, and buses connect different parts of the valley, providing access to various outdoor activities and sightseeing spots.

TRAVEL PLANNER

DESTINATION:

DATES:

FLIGHT DETAILS:

MON	TUES	WED	THURS	FRI	SAT	SUN

SIGHTS TO SEE:

PLACES TO EAT:

EXCURSIONS:

FLIGHT DETAILS:

PAMELA COUTLER

TRAVEL PLANNER

TRAVEL PLANNER

DESTINATION:

DATES:

MON	TUES	WED	THURS	FRI	SAT	SUN

SIGHTS TO SEE: ----------------------

PLACES TO EAT: ----------------------

EXCURSIONS: ----------------------

FLIGHT DETAILS:

PAMELA COUTLER

CHAPTER TWO:

EXPLORING CHAMONIX TOWN

Charming Chamonix: A Town Overview

Chamonix stands as a picturesque alpine town, enchanting visitors with its unique blend of natural beauty, rich history, and vibrant atmosphere. This town overview provides insight into the captivating essence of Chamonix, highlighting its key features and inviting charm.

Historic Streets and Architecture:

Chamonix's heart reveals itself through its charming historic streets, lined with traditional alpine chalets adorned with wooden facades and flower-covered balconies.

The town's architecture exudes a timeless charm, where each building seems to tell a story of its own. The Church of Saint-Michel, an 18th-century architectural gem, and the Maison de la Montagne add to the historical allure.

Town Squares and Cafés:

Chamonix's town squares are lively hubs that come alive with the energy of locals and visitors alike. Place Balmat and Place du Triangle de l'Amitié are central gathering spots surrounded by cozy cafés and bistros.

Sidewalk terraces provide the perfect vantage point to soak in the alpine ambiance, sipping on a warm beverage while taking in views of the surrounding peaks.

Shopping Districts:

The town boasts a vibrant shopping scene with boutique stores offering a curated selection of alpine-inspired fashion, outdoor gear, and local crafts.

Rue du Docteur Paccard, Chamonix's main shopping street, is a delightful avenue to explore, featuring an array of shops where visitors can find unique souvenirs and gifts.

Culinary Delights:

Chamonix is a haven for food enthusiasts, offering a diverse culinary landscape that ranges from cozy mountain-side cafés to fine dining establishments. Savoyard cuisine takes center stage, featuring delectable dishes like fondue, raclette, and hearty mountain fare. Visitors can savor these delights while enjoying panoramic views of the surrounding peaks.

Nightlife and Entertainment:

As the sun sets behind the alpine peaks, Chamonix transforms into a lively nightlife destination. The town offers a variety of bars, pubs, and clubs where visitors can unwind after a day of exploration. Live music, themed nights, and a warm après-ski atmosphere create an inviting ambiance for socializing and making memories.

Art and Culture:

Chamonix's cultural scene is enriched by art galleries, exhibitions, and events that celebrate the town's connection to the Alps. The Alpine Museum showcases the region's mountaineering history, while local artists contribute to the vibrant cultural tapestry.

Community and Festivals:

Chamonix's welcoming community spirit is evident in its festivals and events. Traditional alpine festivals, such as the Ultra-Trail du Mont-Blanc and the Musilac Mont-Blanc music festival, bring together locals and visitors in celebration of the town's dynamic spirit.

Chamonix, with its charming streets, alpine architecture, and warm community vibe, is not just a destination; it's an experience that captivates the senses and lingers in the hearts of those who venture into its mountain embrace.

This town overview offers a glimpse into the soul of Chamonix, inviting travelers to explore its hidden corners and create lasting memories in the embrace of the French Alps.

Iconic Landmarks and Architecture

Chamonix Mont-Blanc, a town nestled in the heart of the French Alps, boasts a rich tapestry of iconic landmarks and architectural gems that reflect its alpine heritage and mountaineering legacy.

1. **Church of Saint-Michel:**

The Church of Saint-Michel, dating back to the 18th century, stands as a prominent landmark in Chamonix. Its Baroque architecture and elegant steeple add to the town's historical charm. Visitors are welcomed by intricate woodwork, stained glass windows, and a serene atmosphere that provides a glimpse into Chamonix's cultural past.

2. Maison de la Montagne:

The Maison de la Montagne, or the House of the Mountain, is another architectural gem that plays a vital role in Chamonix's mountaineering history. This distinctive building, adorned with alpine motifs, serves as a hub for information on mountaineering, hiking, and outdoor activities. It also houses the Chamonix Guides Company, the oldest in the world, offering a connection to the town's adventurous spirit.

3. Place Balmat and the Fountain:

The central square of Place Balmat pays homage to Jacques Balmat, one of the first climbers to ascend

Mont-Blanc. A statue of Balmat stands proudly in the square, surrounded by charming cafés and shops. The nearby Fountain of Tairraz, an ornate water fountain, adds a touch of elegance to the surroundings.

4. Montenvers Railway and Mer de Glace:

The Montenvers Railway, an iconic cogwheel train, takes visitors on a scenic journey to the Mer de Glace, one of the largest glaciers in Europe.

The railway station, with its rustic charm, and the Grand Hotel du Montenvers offer architectural echoes of a bygone era, providing a nostalgic backdrop to the glacial wonder.

5. **Aiguille du Midi and the Cable Car Station:**

The Aiguille du Midi cable car station is a marvel of engineering, perched at an altitude of 3,842 meters (12,605 feet). Its avant-garde design allows visitors to access unparalleled panoramic views of the Alps.

The cable car station itself, a blend of modernity and functionality, stands as a testament to Chamonix's commitment to providing unique mountain experiences.

6. **Rue du Docteur Paccard:**

Chamonix's main shopping street, Rue du Docteur Paccard, is a charming avenue lined with traditional alpine buildings. This bustling street not only serves as a vibrant shopping district but also provides a showcase of architectural styles, from quaint chalets to stylish boutiques.

7. **Chalet des Enfants:**

The Chalet des Enfants, a beautiful wooden building with alpine detailing, is home to the Chamonix Tourist Office. Its warm ambiance and traditional architecture make it a welcoming introduction to the town for visitors.

These iconic landmarks and architectural treasures contribute to the unique character of Chamonix Mont-Blanc. Each structure tells a story of alpine adventure, cultural heritage, and a town deeply connected to the majestic peaks that surround it. As visitors explore these landmarks, they not only witness architectural beauty but also gain insight into Chamonix's profound relationship with the mountains.

Local Cuisine and Dining Recommendations

Chamonix Mont-Blanc, nestled in the French Alps, not only captivates with its stunning landscapes but also offers a delightful culinary experience. The town's local cuisine is deeply rooted in Savoyard traditions, featuring hearty mountain fare that warms the soul after a day of alpine adventures.

1. Fondue Savoyarde:

A quintessential Savoyard dish, Fondue Savoyarde is a communal delight that brings people together around a pot of melted cheese. Emmental and Comté cheeses are commonly used, blended with white wine, garlic, and a hint of nutmeg. Diners dip pieces of bread into the gooey mixture, creating a convivial atmosphere that perfectly complements the mountain setting.

2. Raclette:

Raclette is another cheesy masterpiece that graces Chamonix's dining tables. This dish involves melting a wheel of Raclette cheese and scraping the gooey goodness onto potatoes, cured meats, and pickles. The result is a savory symphony that embodies the heartiness of alpine cuisine.

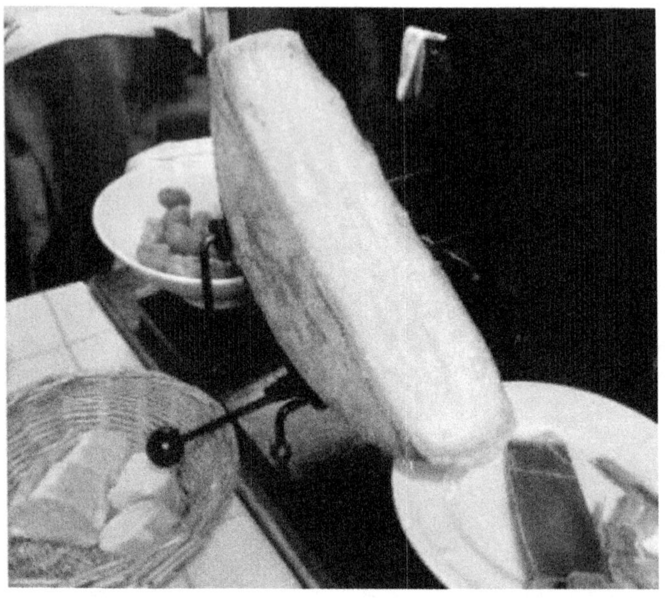

3. Tartiflette:

Originating from the Savoie region, Tartiflette is a comforting casserole featuring layers of potatoes, reblochon cheese, lardons (bacon), and onions.

Baked to golden perfection, this dish is a delightful blend of creamy, cheesy, and smoky flavors that resonate with the alpine spirit.

4. Diots au Vin Blanc:

For those craving a taste of local sausages, Diots au Vin Blanc is a must-try. These Savoyard sausages are simmered in white wine, creating a savory and flavorful dish. Often served with polenta or potatoes, Diots au Vin Blanc is a hearty option that showcases the region's culinary craftsmanship.

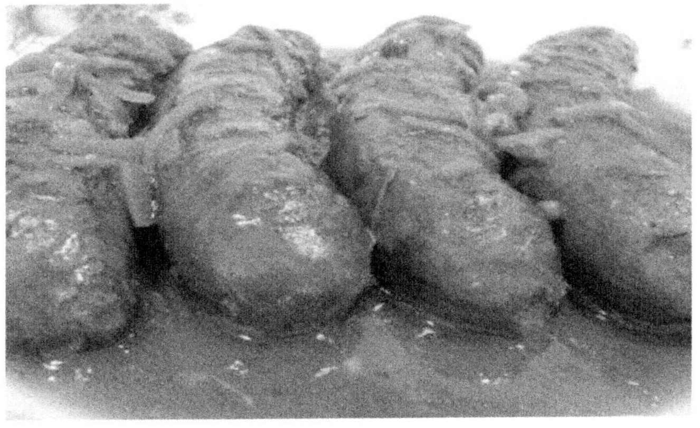

5. **Poulet aux Morilles:**

Poulet aux Morilles, or chicken with morel mushrooms, is a delicacy that highlights the abundance of local ingredients. The earthy flavors of morel mushrooms complement the tender chicken, creating a sophisticated dish that reflects the culinary finesse of Chamonix.

6. **Local Cheeses:**

Chamonix is surrounded by dairy-rich regions, and the local cheeses are a testament to this abundance. Beaufort, Reblochon, Abondance, and Tomme de Savoie are just a few varieties that grace the cheeseboards of Chamonix. Pair them with crusty bread and local honey for a delightful culinary experience.

7. **Mountain Side Cafés and Bakeries:**

Exploring the town's charming streets will lead you to mountain-side cafés and bakeries offering delectable pastries, cakes, and hot beverages. Indulge in a croissant or a slice of tarte aux myrtilles (blueberry tart) while enjoying panoramic views of the surrounding peaks.

8. **Fine Dining Restaurants:**

Chamonix also boasts fine dining establishments where chefs showcase their culinary expertise. These restaurants offer creative interpretations of traditional dishes, often using locally sourced and seasonal ingredients to craft memorable dining experiences.

From cozy mountain huts to elegant restaurants, Chamonix's culinary scene is as diverse as its landscapes. Whether savoring classic Savoyard dishes or exploring modern interpretations of alpine cuisine, dining in Chamonix is an integral part of the overall mountain experience.

Shopping Districts and Souvenirs

Chamonix Mont-Blanc, nestled in the French Alps, is not only a haven for outdoor enthusiasts but also offers a charming shopping experience with a range of boutique stores, alpine markets, and specialty shops. Here's a detailed exploration of the shopping districts and the unique souvenirs that contribute to the town's vibrant atmosphere.

1. Rue du Docteur Paccard:

The main shopping street, Rue du Docteur Paccard, is the bustling heart of Chamonix's retail scene. This pedestrian-friendly avenue is lined with an array of shops, boutiques, and galleries, creating a lively atmosphere for visitors. Here, you can find everything from stylish alpine fashion and outdoor gear to local crafts and souvenirs.

2. Chamonix Market:

For a taste of local flavors and artisanal products, the Chamonix market is a must-visit. Held regularly, the market showcases a variety of fresh produce, cheeses, handmade crafts, and regional specialties. It's an ideal place to pick up authentic local ingredients or unique handmade souvenirs.

3. Chamonix-Made Souvenirs:

Chamonix offers a range of souvenirs that reflect the town's alpine charm. Look for items crafted by local artisans, such as handmade wooden carvings, traditional Savoyard pottery, and intricately designed textiles. These unique souvenirs provide a tangible connection to Chamonix's cultural heritage.

4. **Alpine Fashion Boutiques:**

Chamonix's fashion scene is influenced by its alpine surroundings, offering a mix of chic and practical attire. Explore boutique stores that showcase stylish alpine fashion, including cozy knitwear, durable outdoor gear, and accessories designed to withstand the mountain climate.

5. Chocolateries and Patisseries:

Indulge your taste buds in Chamonix's chocolateries and patisseries, where you'll find delectable treats and gourmet delights. Local chocolates, pastries, and artisanal sweets make for delicious souvenirs or delightful gifts to bring back home.

6. Sports and Outdoor Gear Shops:

Given Chamonix's reputation as an outdoor adventure hub, the town is dotted with sports and outdoor gear shops. Whether you're in need of high-quality hiking equipment, skiing gear, or mountaineering essentials, these specialized stores cater to both beginners and seasoned adventurers.

7. **Art Galleries and Photography Studios:**

Chamonix's stunning landscapes have inspired artists and photographers for centuries. Explore the town's art galleries and photography studios to discover captivating visual representations of the surrounding mountains.

Artwork and prints make for unique and meaningful souvenirs that capture the essence of Chamonix.

8. Local Bookstores and Libraries:

Immerse yourself in the town's rich mountaineering history by exploring local bookstores and libraries. Here, you can find a collection of literature dedicated to alpine adventures, as well as guidebooks, maps, and memoirs that offer insights into the region.

Navigating Chamonix's shopping districts provides an opportunity to not only find unique souvenirs but also to immerse yourself in the vibrant culture and craftsmanship of the French Alps. From fashionable boutiques to quaint markets, Chamonix's diverse retail landscape caters to every taste and interest.

Nightlife and Entertainment

Chamonix Mont-Blanc, renowned for its breathtaking landscapes by day, transforms into a lively and vibrant destination at night. The town offers a diverse array of nightlife and entertainment options, catering to a spectrum of tastes and preferences.

1. Après-Ski Scene:

Chamonix's nightlife kicks off with the après-ski scene, a tradition deeply embedded in alpine culture. As the sun sets behind the majestic peaks, skiers and snowboarders gather at the slopeside bars and mountain huts to unwind. Enjoy a well-deserved drink, often accompanied by live music, while basking in the warm glow of the setting sun on the snow-covered mountains.

2. **Bars and Pubs:**

Chamonix boasts a lively selection of bars and pubs that cater to a diverse crowd. From intimate wine bars to bustling pubs, each venue has its own character and ambiance. Le Choucas, an iconic apres-ski bar, and the Monkey Bar, known for its vibrant atmosphere, are popular choices for those seeking a social and energetic night out.

3. Live Music Venues:

For music enthusiasts, Chamonix offers live music venues that host local and international artists. Le Cab'Anes and The Jekyll & Hyde Pub often feature live performances ranging from acoustic sets to energetic bands, creating an electrifying atmosphere for patrons to enjoy.

4. Clubs and Late-Night Venues:

As the night progresses, Chamonix's nightlife evolves to include clubs and late-night venues. Amnesia Club, with its pulsating beats and energetic vibe, is a popular choice for those looking to dance into the early hours.

These venues often host themed nights, DJ sets, and special events to keep the energy high.

5. **Cinemas and Cultural Events:**

Chamonix offers cultural entertainment beyond the bars and clubs. The town's cinema, Cinéma Vox, screens a mix of international and local films.

Additionally, Chamonix hosts cultural events, film festivals, and art exhibitions, providing a more relaxed and intellectually stimulating form of entertainment.

6. Casino and Games:

For those feeling lucky, Casino Barrière Chamonix offers a sophisticated gaming experience. Try your hand at poker, roulette, or slot machines in an elegant setting. The casino also hosts events and shows, adding an element of glamour to Chamonix's nightlife.

7. **Themed Nights and Special Events:**

Chamonix's nightlife calendar is punctuated with themed nights and special events. From costume parties to themed DJ nights, these events add a playful and dynamic element to the town's entertainment scene. Keep an eye on local event calendars for information on upcoming festivities.

Whether you prefer a cozy evening in a wine bar, dancing until dawn in a nightclub, or enjoying live music in an intimate venue, Chamonix's nightlife ensures that every night out is a memorable experience. The vibrant energy of the town, coupled with the stunning backdrop of the Alps, creates a nightlife and entertainment scene that complements the thrill of the mountains.

TRAVEL PLANNER

TRAVEL PLANNER

DESTINATION:

DATES:

MON	TUES	WED	THURS	FRI	SAT	SUN

SIGHTS TO SEE:

PLACES TO EAT:

EXCURSIONS:

FLIGHT DETAILS:

PAMELA COUTLER

TRAVEL PLANNER

DESTINATION:

DATES:

FLIGHT DETAILS:

MON	TUES	WED	THURS	FRI	SAT	SUN

SIGHTS TO SEE:

PLACES TO EAT:

EXCURSIONS:

FLIGHT DETAILS:

PAMELA COUTLER

CHAPTER THREE:

OUTDOOR ADVENTURES IN THE MONT-BLANC REGION

Mont-Blanc Massif: A Natural Marvel

The Mont-Blanc Massif, an awe-inspiring mountain range situated in the heart of the French Alps, stands as a natural marvel and a testament to the grandeur of Mother Nature. This massif, often referred to as the "White Mountain," is dominated by Mont-Blanc, Western Europe's highest peak, and encompasses a collection of towering summits, glaciers, and breathtaking landscapes.

Geographical Features:

The Mont-Blanc Massif extends across the borders of France, Italy, and Switzerland, creating a majestic alpine panorama. The massif covers a vast area, and its geological formations showcase the dynamic forces that shaped the landscape over millennia. Rugged cliffs, deep valleys, and pristine alpine meadows characterize this region, providing a diverse and visually stunning environment.

Mont-Blanc:

At the heart of the massif stands Mont-Blanc, reaching an impressive elevation of 4,810 meters (15,781 feet) above sea level. The iconic peak is a beacon for mountaineers and outdoor enthusiasts worldwide, attracting climbers seeking the ultimate alpine challenge. Mont-Blanc's snow-covered summit offers panoramic views that stretch across the French, Italian, and Swiss Alps, creating a breathtaking spectacle for those who venture to its heights.

Glaciers and Icefields:

The Mont-Blanc Massif is home to a network of glaciers, including the famous Mer de Glace, which translates to "Sea of Ice." These immense icefields flow down the valleys, shaping the terrain and providing a stark contrast to the rugged rock formations. The glaciers are not only awe-inspiring to behold but also play a crucial role in regulating water flow in the region.

Flora and Fauna:

Despite the challenging alpine conditions, the Mont-Blanc Massif supports a remarkable array of flora and fauna. Alpine meadows burst into bloom during the short summer months, showcasing a vibrant palette of wildflowers. Marmots, chamois, ibex, and golden eagles are among the resilient animal species that have adapted to the harsh alpine environment, adding life to the dramatic landscape.

Outdoor Activities:

The Mont-Blanc Massif serves as a playground for outdoor enthusiasts, offering a myriad of activities throughout the year. In winter, the region transforms into a winter sports haven, with world-renowned ski resorts such as Chamonix attracting skiers and snowboarders. In summer, the massif becomes a paradise for hikers, climbers, and mountaineers, each trail providing a unique perspective on the natural beauty of the Alps.

Conservation and Sustainability:

Recognizing the ecological importance of the Mont-Blanc Massif, efforts have been made to preserve and protect its fragile ecosystem. Conservation initiatives and sustainable practices aim to ensure the longevity of this natural marvel, striking a delicate balance between human enjoyment and environmental preservation.

The Mont-Blanc Massif stands as a testament to the captivating power of nature, captivating those who explore its heights and valleys. Its pristine beauty, challenging terrain, and ecological significance make it a natural marvel that continues to inspire awe and reverence for the wonders of the alpine world.

Hiking and Trekking Trails

Chamonix Mont-Blanc, surrounded by the majestic peaks of the French Alps, is a haven for hiking and trekking enthusiasts. The region offers a diverse network of trails that cater to all levels of experience, providing breathtaking vistas, alpine meadows, and access to some of the most iconic summits in Europe. Here's a detailed exploration of the hiking and trekking trails that make Chamonix a paradise for outdoor adventurers.

1. **Tour du Mont-Blanc (TMB):**

The crown jewel of trekking in Chamonix is the Tour du Mont-Blanc, a classic long-distance trail that circumnavigates the entire Mont-Blanc Massif. This multi-day trek spans a distance of roughly 165 kilometres (103 mi) with 10 kilometres (6.2 mi) of ascent/descent and passing through parts of Switzerland, Italy and France. Hikers are treated to ever-changing landscapes, quaint alpine villages, and close-up views of the towering peaks.

2. **Aiguilles Rouges Nature Reserve:**

On the opposite side of the Chamonix Valley lies the Aiguilles Rouges Nature Reserve, offering a plethora of hiking trails amid stunning red-tinged peaks. Trails like the Lac Blanc hike provide panoramic views of Mont-Blanc and access to pristine mountain lakes. The Aiguilles Rouges trails cater to varying skill levels, making it an accessible area for both novice and experienced hikers.

3. **Brevent-Flegere Loop:**

For those seeking a challenging day hike, the Brevent-Flegere Loop is a popular choice. Starting from

Chamonix, the trail takes you up the Brevent cable car, offering spectacular views of Mont-Blanc. The loop then traverses scenic ridges, providing an immersive alpine experience before descending to the Flegere cable car.

4. **Lac Cornu and Lacs Noirs:**

A moderate trek takes you to the stunning Lac Cornu and Lacs Noirs, nestled amid the Mont-Blanc Massif. The trail weaves through alpine meadows and rocky terrain, culminating in the breathtaking sight of turquoise mountain lakes surrounded by rugged peaks.

This hike is perfect for those looking for a rewarding day trip.

5. **Grand Balcon Nord:**

The Grand Balcon Nord trail offers a picturesque traverse along the northern side of the Chamonix Valley. Hikers are treated to sweeping views of the Aiguille du Midi, Mont-Blanc, and the Bossons Glacier.

The trail can be customized to different lengths, making it suitable for a variety of fitness levels.

6. La Jonction:

La Jonction is a challenging trek that ventures into the heart of the Mont-Blanc Massif. Starting at the Mer de Glace, the trail ascends through rocky terrain and alpine landscapes, ultimately reaching a stunning viewpoint where two glaciers meet.

This trek provides a close encounter with the glacial wonders of the region.

7. Plan de l'Aiguille to Montenvers:

For a relatively easier hike, the trail from Plan de l'Aiguille to Montenvers offers breathtaking views of the Mer de Glace and the surrounding peaks. Accessible via the Aiguille du Midi cable car, this trail is a perfect introduction to the alpine environment.

Trail Difficulty and Safety:

Chamonix's hiking and trekking trails cater to a range of difficulty levels, from gentle walks for beginners to challenging ascents for seasoned mountaineers. It's essential to be well-prepared, check trail conditions, and adhere to safety guidelines, especially in higher-altitude areas where weather conditions can change rapidly.

Chamonix Mont-Blanc's hiking and trekking trails not only showcase the region's natural beauty but also offer a profound connection to the rich alpine heritage. Whether exploring glacial landscapes, traversing ridges, or embarking on a multi-day trek, each trail in Chamonix promises an unforgettable adventure in the heart of the French Alps.

Skiing and Snowboarding Opportunities

Chamonix Mont-Blanc, often referred to as the "Capital of Extreme Sports," is a world-renowned destination for skiing and snowboarding. Surrounded by the iconic peaks of the French Alps, the region offers a diverse range of slopes, off-piste terrain, and breathtaking alpine scenery, making it a paradise for winter sports enthusiasts. Here's a detailed exploration of the skiing and snowboarding opportunities that make Chamonix a premier destination for snow lovers.

1. Chamonix Ski Resorts:

Chamonix boasts several ski resorts that cater to a variety of skill levels. The Chamonix-Mont-Blanc ski area is the largest, offering an extensive network of slopes, including gentle runs for beginners and challenging descents for advanced skiers and snowboarders. Other notable resorts in the area include Les Houches, Le Tour, and Grand Montets, each with its unique charm and terrain.

2. Vallée Blanche Off-Piste Descent:

For experienced skiers and snowboarders seeking an adrenaline rush, the Vallée Blanche off-piste descent is an iconic adventure. Accessed via the Aiguille du Midi cable car, this high-mountain route provides stunning views of the Mont-Blanc massif. The descent, surrounded by glacial landscapes, takes you through challenging snowfields and offers an unforgettable backcountry experience.

3. Aiguille du Midi and La Vallée Blanche:

The Aiguille du Midi cable car, often dubbed the "Top of Europe," serves as a gateway to some of the best off-piste opportunities. Skiers and snowboarders can access La Vallée Blanche from the Aiguille du Midi station, embarking on a thrilling descent through glacial terrain. This iconic route is a must for those seeking adventure beyond the groomed slopes.

4. Freeride and Backcountry Terrain:

Chamonix is renowned for its extensive freeride and backcountry terrain. Enthusiasts can explore ungroomed slopes, powder-filled bowls, and challenging couloirs. Local guides and instructors are available for those looking to enhance their skills and safely navigate the exciting off-piste offerings.

5. Snowparks and Freestyle Areas:

Chamonix doesn't only cater to the seasoned skier or snowboarder; it also provides opportunities for freestyle enthusiasts. The Grands Montets snowpark is a hub for freestyle riders, featuring jumps, rails, and other elements. It's an excellent spot for honing tricks and enjoying a playful day on the slopes.

6. Ski and Snowboard Schools:

For beginners or those looking to improve their skills, Chamonix offers reputable ski and snowboard schools. Certified instructors provide lessons tailored to individual abilities, ensuring a safe and enjoyable learning experience. Private lessons and group classes are available, allowing participants to progress at their own pace.

7. Ski Touring and Splitboarding:

Chamonix's backcountry is a haven for ski touring and splitboarding. Adventure seekers can explore untouched snowfields, ascend mountain slopes, and experience the tranquility of the alpine wilderness. Various routes, such as the Haute Route, provide unforgettable journeys for those seeking a more immersive mountain experience.

Safety and Equipment:

While Chamonix offers unparalleled skiing and snowboarding experiences, it's crucial to prioritize safety. Always check weather and avalanche conditions, wear appropriate gear, and consider hiring a guide for off-piste adventures. The town's numerous rental shops provide quality equipment, ensuring that visitors have the right gear for their chosen activities.

Chamonix Mont-Blanc's skiing and snowboarding opportunities are not merely a winter pastime; they are a thrilling exploration of the breathtaking landscapes that have drawn adventure seekers for generations. From the groomed slopes of its renowned resorts to the untamed backcountry, Chamonix continues to be a beacon for those seeking the ultimate winter sports adventure in the heart of the French Alps.

Climbing and Mountaineering Experiences

Chamonix Mont-Blanc, often hailed as the "Mountaineering Capital of the World," is a mecca for climbers and mountaineers. Nestled in the heart of the French Alps, the region boasts some of the most iconic peaks and challenging ascents, offering a diverse range of climbing and mountaineering experiences. Here's a detailed exploration of the opportunities that make Chamonix a premier destination for those seeking the thrill of the vertical world.

1. **Mont-Blanc Summit Ascent:**

The crowning achievement for mountaineers in Chamonix is the ascent of Mont-Blanc, the highest peak in Western Europe at 4,810 meters (15,781 feet). Climbing Mont-Blanc requires a combination of technical skill, physical endurance, and acclimatization. Various routes, such as the Gouter Route and the Three Monts Route, provide different challenges and awe-inspiring views.

2. **Aiguille du Midi:**

The Aiguille du Midi, accessible by cable car, serves as a gateway to numerous mountaineering routes. Climbers can explore challenging ascents, such as the Cosmiques Arete or the Mallory-Porter route, which lead to panoramic views of the Mont-Blanc massif. The Aiguille du Midi also provides access to the Vallée Blanche for those seeking a high-altitude glacier experience.

3. Glacier Travel and Ice Climbing:

Chamonix's glaciated terrain offers opportunities for glacier travel and ice climbing. The Mer de Glace, one of the largest glaciers in the Alps, provides a unique setting for learning and practicing glacier travel skills.

For ice climbing enthusiasts, the surrounding valleys offer frozen waterfalls and cascades, creating a playground for those seeking vertical ice challenges.

4. **Chamonix Aiguilles and Rock Climbing:**

The Aiguilles (needles) surrounding Chamonix present a playground for rock climbers. From classic multi-pitch routes to challenging technical climbs, these granite spires offer a variety of rock climbing experiences. The Aiguille du Plan, Aiguille de l'M, and Aiguille de l'Index are just a few of the iconic peaks that attract climbers from around the world.

5. **Climbing Schools and Guides:**

For those new to climbing or seeking guidance in the alpine environment, Chamonix is home to reputable climbing schools and mountain guides. These professionals provide instruction in rock climbing, ice climbing, and mountaineering techniques. Guided climbs offer a safe and educational way to explore the region's challenging terrain.

6. Haute Route and Alpine Trekking:

The Haute Route, a classic high-altitude trek, takes adventurers from Chamonix to Zermatt, traversing stunning alpine landscapes. While not a technical climb, the Haute Route involves challenging terrain, high mountain passes, and unforgettable alpine vistas. It is a favorite among those seeking an extended mountaineering adventure.

7. Alpine Bivouacs and Huts:

To fully immerse in the mountaineering experience, climbers can stay in alpine bivouacs or mountain huts. These shelters are strategically located along popular routes, providing a place to rest and acclimatize. Overnight stays in these huts offer a unique opportunity to experience the mountain environment and connect with fellow climbers.

Safety and Preparation:

Climbing and mountaineering in Chamonix require careful preparation and attention to safety. Weather conditions can change rapidly, and the high-altitude environment poses unique challenges. It's essential to be physically fit, acclimatized, and well-equipped with proper gear. Engaging with local guides and schools ensures a safe and enjoyable mountaineering experience.

Chamonix Mont-Blanc's climbing and mountaineering experiences are not merely physical challenges; they are immersive journeys into the heart of the Alps. From the iconic peaks to the glaciated landscapes, Chamonix continues to inspire climbers and mountaineers, offering a world-class playground for those who seek the heights of adventure.

Paragliding, Rafting, and Other Adventure Sports

Chamonix Mont-Blanc, known for its towering peaks and alpine landscapes, is not only a destination for mountaineers but also an adventure playground offering a myriad of thrilling activities. From soaring high above the valleys with paragliding to navigating the tumultuous rivers through white-water rafting, Chamonix provides a diverse range of adventure sports that cater to adrenaline seekers. Here's a detailed exploration of paragliding, rafting, and other exciting activities that make Chamonix a haven for adventure enthusiasts.

1. **Paragliding:**

Soar like a bird above the stunning Chamonix Valley with paragliding. Tandem paragliding experiences allow participants to take to the skies in the company of experienced pilots. Launching from high-altitude sites such as Brevent or Planpraz, participants enjoy panoramic views of Mont-Blanc, Aiguille du Midi, and the surrounding peaks. The sensation of gliding through the air provides a unique perspective on the alpine landscapes.

2. **White-Water Rafting:**

Chamonix's rivers, fed by melting glaciers, offer exhilarating white-water rafting experiences. Navigate through the twists and turns of the Arve and Dranse rivers, battling rapids and enjoying the rush of cold mountain water. Rafting excursions cater to various skill levels, making it accessible for both beginners and experienced rafters.

3. **Via Ferrata:**

For those seeking a vertical adventure, Chamonix's via ferrata routes provide a thrilling combination of rock climbing and hiking. Secured to steel cables, climbers traverse rock faces and suspension bridges, offering a unique way to explore the high mountain environment. Popular routes include the Curalla Via Ferrata and the Saix du Tour.

4. Canyoning:

Explore the hidden corners of Chamonix's valleys through canyoning adventures. Descend through narrow gorges, slide down natural chutes, and rappel beside waterfalls.

Canyoning excursions combine elements of hiking, climbing, and swimming, providing a refreshing and adventurous way to experience the region's diverse terrain.

5. **Rock Climbing:**

Chamonix's granite spires and crags make it an ideal destination for rock climbing enthusiasts. Whether scaling the Aiguilles or exploring the numerous climbing areas in the surrounding valleys, rock climbers have a wealth of options.

Climbing schools and guides are available for both beginners and experienced climbers seeking to conquer Chamonix's vertical challenges.

6. Mountain Biking:

Discover Chamonix's rugged trails and scenic landscapes on two wheels with mountain biking. From downhill trails to cross-country routes, the region offers a variety of biking experiences.

Lift-accessed bike parks, such as Le Tour and Les Houches, provide thrilling descents, while the network of alpine trails caters to all levels of riders.

7. **Skydiving:**

For the ultimate adrenaline rush, experience the thrill of freefall with skydiving. Soar above the Chamonix Valley, taking in panoramic views of the Mont-Blanc massif before leaping into the sky.

Tandem skydiving provides an accessible way for participants to enjoy the sensation of freefall with the guidance of a certified instructor.

8. Hot Air Ballooning:

For a more serene adventure, embark on a hot air balloon ride over the Chamonix Valley. Drift peacefully above the landscapes, taking in the breathtaking views of the mountains, glaciers, and valleys. Hot air ballooning provides a unique and tranquil way to appreciate the beauty of the region.

Safety and Guided Tours:

Participating in adventure sports in Chamonix requires careful consideration of safety. Many activities are offered through guided tours or schools with experienced instructors. It's essential to adhere to safety guidelines, use proper equipment, and choose activities that match individual skill levels.

Chamonix Mont-Blanc's diverse array of adventure sports goes beyond the traditional alpine pursuits. Whether soaring through the air with paragliding, conquering rapids with white-water rafting, or exploring via ferrata routes, adventurers find an abundance of exhilarating experiences against the backdrop of the French Alps.

TRAVEL PLANNER

TRAVEL PLANNER

DESTINATION:

DATES:

MON	TUES	WED	THURS	FRI	SAT	SUN

SIGHTS TO SEE:

PLACES TO EAT:

EXCURSIONS:

FLIGHT DETAILS:

PAMELA COUTLER

TRAVEL PLANNER

DESTINATION:

DATES:

MON	TUES	WED	THURS	FRI	SAT	SUN

SIGHTS TO SEE:

PLACES TO EAT:

EXCURSIONS:

FLIGHT DETAILS:

PAMELA COUTLER

CHAPTER FOUR:

CULTURAL AND HISTORICAL DELIGHTS

Museums and Art Galleries

Chamonix Mont-Blanc, renowned for its breathtaking natural beauty and thrilling outdoor activities, also offers a cultural haven with a range of museums and art galleries. These institutions provide a deeper understanding of the region's history, mountaineering heritage, and the artistic expressions inspired by the alpine landscapes. Here's a detailed exploration of the museums and art galleries that enrich the cultural fabric of Chamonix.

1. Musée Alpin Chamonix

Located in the heart of Chamonix, the Alpine Museum is a treasure trove of artifacts, documents, and exhibits that delve into the rich history of mountaineering in the region. The museum showcases the evolution of alpine exploration, the development of climbing techniques, and the stories of legendary mountaineers who have conquered the peaks of the Mont-Blanc massif.

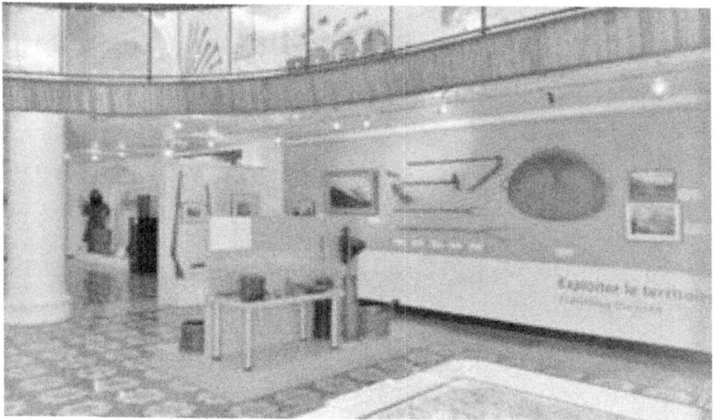

2. Musée des Cristaux (Crystal Museum):

Nestled within the Aiguille du Midi cable car complex, the Crystal Museum is a fascinating showcase of minerals and crystals found in the Mont-Blanc massif.

Visitors can marvel at the dazzling array of specimens, including quartz, fluorite, and tourmaline, highlighting the geological wonders of the region.

3. Maison de la Mémoire et du Patrimoine - Marcel Wibault (House of Memory and Heritage):

This museum, located in Les Houches near Chamonix, celebrates the life and work of Marcel Wibault, an artist and passionate advocate for the preservation of mountain heritage.

The museum displays his sculptures, paintings, and writings, offering a unique perspective on the cultural significance of the Alps.

4. **Art Galleries in Chamonix Center:**

Stroll through the charming streets of Chamonix Center to discover an array of boutique art galleries. These intimate spaces showcase local and international artists, presenting a diverse selection of paintings, sculptures, and contemporary artworks. Visitors can immerse themselves in the creative atmosphere and explore the art scene of the town.

5. **Musée Montagnard (Mountain Museum) in Les Houches:**

Located in Les Houches, just a short distance from Chamonix, the Mountain Museum provides insight into the traditional alpine way of life.

The museum exhibits artifacts, tools, and crafts that depict the history of mountain communities, showcasing the resilience and resourcefulness of those who have called the Alps home.

Chamonix Mont-Blanc's museums and art galleries offer a cultural counterpoint to the outdoor adventures that define the region. Whether exploring the history of mountaineering, admiring crystals, or immersing oneself in contemporary art, these institutions contribute to the rich tapestry of Chamonix's cultural heritage.

Historical Sites and Monuments

Chamonix Mont-Blanc, celebrated for its stunning natural landscapes, also harbors a rich historical heritage that is reflected in its architectural gems and historical sites. These monuments bear witness to the town's evolution from a quaint mountain village to a globally recognized destination for outdoor enthusiasts. Here's a detailed exploration of the historical sites and monuments that tell the story of Chamonix's past.

1. Château de Saint-Michel:

Perched on a hill overlooking the Chamonix Valley, Château de Saint-Michel is a medieval castle that dates back to the 14th century.

Originally built as a defensive structure, the castle has witnessed centuries of history. Visitors can explore the well-preserved ruins and enjoy panoramic views of the surrounding mountains.

2. Church of Saint Michel:

Adjacent to Château de Saint-Michel, the Church of Saint Michel is a religious monument that has stood since the 18th century.

This Baroque-style church features ornate decorations, intricate woodwork, and beautiful stained glass windows. The church adds a touch of historical charm to the village and stands as a testament to the religious and cultural history of Chamonix.

3. **Montenvers Railway Station and Mer de Glace:**

The Montenvers Railway, inaugurated in 1908, is a historical cogwheel train that takes visitors to the Montenvers station.

From here, a spectacular panorama unfolds, offering views of the iconic Mer de Glace glacier. The railway and station themselves are historic, providing a glimpse into the early days of tourism in the Chamonix Valley.

4. **Aiguille du Midi:**

While primarily known as a starting point for mountaineering adventures, the Aiguille du Midi also has historical significance.

The cable car, inaugurated in 1955, was a groundbreaking engineering feat at the time. Visitors can appreciate the historical context and enjoy breathtaking views of the Mont-Blanc massif from the observation terraces.

5. **Drus and Aiguille Verte:**

The towering peaks of Drus and Aiguille Verte are not only icons of Chamonix's skyline but also hold historical significance in the realm of mountaineering.

Climbers and mountaineers have long been drawn to these challenging summits, contributing to the rich history of alpinism in the region.

6. **Belle Époque Architecture:**

Stroll through the streets of Chamonix, and you'll encounter well-preserved examples of Belle Époque architecture. Elegant hotels, charming chalets, and historic buildings showcase the town's development as a popular destination in the late 19th and early 20th centuries.

The Casino Barrière, dating back to 1905, is a notable architectural gem.

7. **Monument to the Guides:**

In the heart of Chamonix, the Monument to the Guides pays tribute to the local mountain guides who have played a pivotal role in the region's mountaineering history. The monument, featuring a bronze statue of a guide with outstretched arms, serves as a poignant reminder of the bravery and skill of these mountain pioneers.

Chamonix Mont-Blanc's historical sites and monuments offer a captivating journey through time, revealing the layers of history that have shaped this alpine town. From medieval castles to Belle Époque architecture, each monument tells a story of Chamonix's evolution while preserving the cultural and historical essence that makes it a unique destination.

Alpine Traditons and Festivals

Chamonix Mont-Blanc, nestled in the heart of the French Alps, is not only a haven for outdoor enthusiasts but also a place deeply rooted in Alpine traditions. Throughout the year, the town comes alive with festivals and celebrations that pay homage to the rich cultural heritage of the region. Here's a detailed exploration of Alpine traditions and festivals that add a vibrant cultural dimension to Chamonix.

1. **La Fête des Guides (The Guides' Festival):**

Celebrated in mid-August, La Fête des Guides is a highlight of Chamonix's calendar, honoring the mountain guides who have played a crucial role in the town's history.

The festival features a colorful parade, traditional costumes, and ceremonies paying tribute to the bravery and skill of the local guides. It's a time when the community comes together to celebrate its mountain heritage.

2. **Transhumance Festival:**

In late June, as the snow melts and alpine meadows come to life, Chamonix hosts the Transhumance

Festival. This celebration marks the seasonal migration of livestock to higher pastures.

Traditional ceremonies, music, and local crafts showcase the agricultural heritage of the region, and participants can witness the spectacle of herds making their way through the town.

3. Christmas Markets and Festivities:

Chamonix transforms into a winter wonderland during the Christmas season. Festive markets, adorned with twinkling lights and surrounded by snow-capped peaks, offer local crafts, delicious treats, and a warm atmosphere.

The Christmas season also brings traditional music, storytelling, and visits from Santa Claus, creating a magical ambiance for residents and visitors alike.

4. **École du Ski Français (ESF) Torchlight Descent:**

In February, the ESF Torchlight Descent illuminates the slopes of Chamonix as ski instructors and participants descend the mountains carrying torches.

This spectacle not only showcases the skill of the local ski school but also pays homage to the age-old tradition of guiding through the mountains with torchlight.

5. **Chamonix Yoga Festival:**

While not strictly an Alpine tradition, the Chamonix Yoga Festival, typically held in July, has become a celebration of wellness amid the stunning alpine scenery. The festival combines yoga classes, mindfulness practices, and outdoor activities, providing a unique blend of holistic well-being against the backdrop of the Mont-Blanc massif.

6. La Musique en l'Été (Music in Summer):

Throughout the summer, Chamonix resonates with the melodies of La Musique en l'Été.

This music festival brings together local and international artists, performing classical, jazz, and contemporary music in various venues across the town. Attendees can enjoy open-air concerts, creating a harmonious atmosphere in the Alpine surroundings.

7. Chamonix International Film Festival:

The Chamonix International Film Festival, held annually, celebrates the art of mountain filmmaking. Documentaries, feature films, and shorts showcase the beauty and challenges of mountain life, as well as the spirit of adventure that defines the Alps.

The festival brings together filmmakers, enthusiasts,

and a diverse audience for a cinematic exploration of alpine culture.

8. Alphorn Festival:

In a nod to traditional Alpine music, the Alphorn Festival gathers musicians from across the region to showcase their skills with this iconic instrument.

The deep tones of the alphorn resonate through the mountains, providing a unique auditory experience that connects modern Chamonix with its age-old alpine heritage.

These Alpine traditions and festivals in Chamonix Mont-Blanc contribute to the town's unique cultural tapestry, blending the old and the new against the backdrop of the majestic mountains. Whether celebrating the prowess of mountain guides, marking the changing seasons, or enjoying music and film, these events bring the community together and provide visitors with a deeper understanding of Chamonix's rich cultural heritage.

Local Arts and Crafts

Chamonix Mont-Blanc, known for its breathtaking alpine landscapes, is also a hub for local arts and crafts that reflect the region's natural beauty and cultural heritage. From traditional handicrafts to contemporary artistic expressions, Chamonix showcases a diverse array of creations. Here's a detailed exploration of the local arts and crafts that contribute to the cultural richness of this mountain town.

1. Woodcarving:

Woodcarving is a traditional craft that thrives in Chamonix, with artisans creating intricate pieces that often depict alpine scenes, wildlife, and local landmarks. Wooden sculptures, furniture, and decorative items showcase the skill of local woodworkers, and visitors can find beautifully carved pieces in boutique shops and markets.

2. **Alpine Pottery:**

Pottery has been a part of alpine culture for centuries, and in Chamonix, local potters craft unique pieces inspired by the surrounding mountains. Hand-thrown bowls, mugs, and decorative items often feature alpine motifs, capturing the essence of the natural environment.

The vibrant glazes used by local potters reflect the colors of the changing seasons.

3. Traditional Textiles:

Chamonix is home to a variety of traditional textiles, including wool and felt products that reflect the region's mountainous climate. Local artisans create cozy blankets, scarves, and clothing items using high-quality natural fibers.

These textiles often incorporate traditional patterns and designs that have been passed down through generations.

4. Jewelry Inspired by Nature:

Local jewelers draw inspiration from the alpine landscape to create unique pieces of jewelry. Designs often feature elements like mountain peaks, pine trees, and snowflakes. The use of locally sourced materials, such as gemstones and crystals, adds a touch of authenticity to these handmade creations.

5. Mountain-inspired Artwork:

Local artists in Chamonix produce a wide range of artwork inspired by the surrounding mountains. Paintings, drawings, and prints often capture the beauty of the Mont-Blanc massif, alpine meadows, and iconic landmarks. These pieces provide a visual celebration of the natural wonders that draw visitors to the region.

6. Leathercraft:

Leathercraft is another traditional skill that local artisans employ to create a variety of items, including belts, wallets, and accessories. The use of high-quality leather and attention to detail result in durable and aesthetically pleasing products that often feature alpine motifs and symbols.

7. **Local Photography:**

Photographers in Chamonix capture the stunning landscapes and dynamic outdoor activities that define the region. Visitors can find a variety of locally produced photographs showcasing the beauty of the French Alps. Many photographers also offer prints, calendars, and books that allow visitors to take a piece of Chamonix's visual splendor home with them.

8. **Contemporary Art Galleries:**

Chamonix boasts contemporary art galleries that feature the works of local and international artists. Paintings, sculptures, and multimedia installations provide a modern perspective on the intersection of art and mountain culture. These galleries contribute to the vibrant art scene and offer a platform for creative expression.

9. **Handcrafted Outdoor Gear:**

Given Chamonix's reputation as an outdoor adventure destination, local artisans often create handcrafted outdoor gear. This includes items like custom-made skis, backpacks, and outdoor apparel. Craftsmanship and attention to detail characterize these products, reflecting the region's passion for outdoor pursuits.

10. **Alpaca Wool Creations:**

With a focus on sustainable and natural materials, some local artisans in Chamonix work with alpaca wool to create soft and luxurious products. Alpaca wool, known for its warmth and durability, is used to craft scarves, hats, and other accessories, providing a cozy reminder of the alpine environment.

Exploring the local arts and crafts in Chamonix Mont-Blanc offers visitors a deeper connection to the region's cultural identity. From traditional crafts that have stood the test of time to contemporary expressions inspired by the mountains, the local artistic scene reflects the diversity and creativity of this alpine community.

Interactions with Local Community

Chamonix Mont-Blanc not only offers breathtaking natural beauty but also a vibrant local community with a rich cultural tapestry. Engaging with the locals can enhance your experience and provide a deeper understanding of the town's history, traditions, and way of life. Here's a detailed exploration of how to interact with the local community in Chamonix.

1. **Participate in Local Festivals:**

Chamonix hosts various festivals and events throughout the year that showcase the town's cultural heritage. Attend La Fête des Guides to celebrate local mountain guides, join in the Transhumance Festival to witness the seasonal migration of livestock, or immerse yourself in Christmas markets and festivities.

These events provide opportunities to interact with locals, enjoy traditional activities, and experience the community spirit.

2. **Attend Local Workshops and Classes:**

Many local artisans and craftsmen in Chamonix offer workshops and classes where you can learn traditional skills such as woodcarving, pottery, or alpine cuisine.

Participating in these activities not only allows you to acquire new skills but also fosters connections with local experts who are passionate about preserving and sharing their craft.

3. Visit Farmers' Markets:

Explore Chamonix's farmers' markets to connect with local producers and artisans. Engage in conversations with farmers, cheese makers, and craftspeople who showcase their products.

The markets offer a glimpse into the agricultural traditions of the region and provide an opportunity to learn about the local produce.

4. Dine in Local Restaurants:

Frequenting local restaurants and cafes is an excellent way to interact with the community and savor authentic Alpine cuisine. Strike up conversations with restaurant owners, chefs, and staff to gain insights into local flavors, ingredients, and culinary traditions.

This personal touch enhances your dining experience and fosters a connection with the community.

5. Join Outdoor Activities and Clubs:

Chamonix's residents are often passionate about outdoor activities. Whether it's skiing, hiking, climbing, or cycling, participating in group activities or joining local clubs provides an avenue to meet like-minded individuals.

This shared love for outdoor pursuits can lead to meaningful connections and a deeper appreciation of the local lifestyle.

6. **Attend Cultural and Art Events:**

Chamonix has a thriving cultural scene with art galleries, music festivals, and performances. Attend exhibitions, concerts, or theater productions to engage with the local arts community.

Artists and performers are often open to discussions about their work, providing insights into the creative aspects of Chamonix's cultural life.

7. **Volunteer for Local Initiatives:**

Volunteering for local environmental, social, or community initiatives is a meaningful way to contribute to the town's well-being and connect with residents.

Whether participating in clean-up events, supporting local charities, or assisting in community projects, volunteering allows you to actively engage with the local community and make a positive impact.

8. Learn the Local Language:

While many locals in Chamonix speak English, making an effort to learn basic French phrases can enhance your interactions.

Locals appreciate visitors who show an interest in their language, and even a few simple greetings can go a long way in fostering connections and breaking down language barriers.

9. Respect Local Customs and Traditions:

Respecting local customs and traditions is crucial for positive interactions. From understanding the etiquette in shops and restaurants to adhering to hiking trail regulations, being mindful of local norms demonstrates cultural sensitivity and helps create a harmonious experience for both visitors and residents.

10. Stay in Local Accommodations:

Opting for local accommodations, such as family-run bed and breakfasts or boutique hotels, provides a more intimate experience and often allows for interactions with the owners and staff.

These hosts can offer insider tips, recommendations, and personal anecdotes that add a personal touch to your stay.

Engaging with the local community in Chamonix Mont-Blanc is not only a way to enhance your travel experience but also an opportunity to gain a deeper appreciation for the town's cultural heritage and the warmth of its residents.

Whether through festivals, workshops, or shared outdoor adventures, connecting with locals adds a valuable dimension to your time in this alpine haven.

MUSILAC
MONT-BLANC
CHAMONIX

TRAVEL PLANNER

DESTINATION: DATES:

MON	TUES	WED	THURS	FRI	SAT	SUN

SIGHTS TO SEE: PLACES TO EAT: EXCURSIONS:

FLIGHT DETAILS:

PAMELA COUTLER

TRAVEL PLANNER

DESTINATION: | DATES:

MON	TUES	WED	THURS	FRI	SAT	SUN

SIGHTS TO SEE: | PLACES TO EAT: | EXCURSIONS:

FLIGHT DETAILS:

PAMELA COUTLER

CHAPTER FIVE:

PRACTICAL INFORMATION AND TRAVEL TIPS

Accommodation Options: Hotels, Chalets, and Hostels

Chamonix Mont-Blanc offers a diverse range of accommodation options to suit the preferences and needs of every traveler. Whether you seek the coziness of a mountain chalet, the comfort of a hotel, or the affordability of a hostel, Chamonix provides a variety of choices for a memorable stay.

i. Hotels:

Chamonix boasts a selection of hotels that cater to different tastes and budgets. From luxury establishments with spa facilities and panoramic mountain views to charming boutique hotels in the town center, visitors can find accommodations that suit their preferences. Many hotels provide convenient access to Chamonix's attractions, shopping areas, and the Aiguille du Midi cable car.

Best Hotels in Chamonix:

i. Hôtel Mont-Blanc:

This upscale hotel sits in Chamonix-Mont-Blanc town center, surrounded by mountains, and is a 10-minute walk from the ski lifts at Brévent.

The airy, modern rooms with light wood accents feature free Wi-Fi, satellite TV and rainfall showers. Many suites add balconies with mountain views; some have private saunas.

There's an elegant French restaurant with an alpine-chic lounge bar and garden seating (seasonal). Other amenities include a heated outdoor pool, a gym, a hot tub and a spa. Shuttle service to nearby ski slopes is complimentary.

Check-in time: 15:00

Check-out time: 11:00

Address & contact information:

62 All. du Majestic, 74400 Chamonix-Mont-Blanc, France

+33 4 50 53 05 64

ii. **Grand Hôtel des Alpes:**

This upscale hotel in the town center is a 9-minute walk from Montenvers Mer de Glace train station, 3.9 km from Golf Club de Chamonix and 600 m from the Le Brévent ski lift.

Plush, classic rooms with marble bathrooms and elegant wood-paneling feature flat-screens, minibars and Wi-Fi; some have balconies and views of Mont Blanc. Suites add whirlpool tubs and living rooms with pull-out sofas.

There's a spa with an indoor pool and a hot tub, plus a sauna, and steam and massage rooms. Breakfast is served in an airy dining room, and there's a refined lounge. A ski-slope shuttle service is available.

Check-in time: 16:00

Check-out time: 12:00

Address & contact information:

75 Rue du Dr Paccard, 74400 Chamonix-Mont-Blanc, France

+33 4 50 55 37 80

ii. Chalets:

For those seeking a more intimate and rustic experience, chalets offer a quintessential alpine atmosphere. These wooden mountain lodgings vary from traditional to modern, providing a cozy retreat after a day of outdoor activities. Chalets can be rented as private accommodations for families or groups, and some include amenities such as fireplaces, hot tubs, and stunning mountain views. Popular chalet options include BlackRock Ski Lodge and Chalet Hôtel Hermitage.

Best Chalets in Chamonix:

i. **Chalet Hotel du Bois:**

Welcome to Chalet Hotel du Bois, your Les Houches "home away from home." Chalet Hotel du Bois aims to make your visit as relaxing and enjoyable as possible, which is why so many guests continue to come back year after year.

You'll enjoy relaxing rooms that offer a flat screen TV and a refrigerator, and you can stay connected during your stay as Chalet Hotel du Bois offers guests free wifi. The hotel features a concierge, room service, and outdoor furniture. Plus, Chalet Hotel du Bois offers a pool and breakfast, providing a pleasant respite from your busy day. For guests with a vehicle, free parking is available.

While in Les Houches be sure to experience local ribs favorites at Le Delice. Chalet Hotel du Bois puts the best of Les Houches at your fingertips, making your stay both relaxing and enjoyable.

Address and Contact Information:

475 avenue des Alpages, 74310 Les Houches, Chamonix France

ii. Le Chalet Hôtel Whymper:

Your new base-camp at the foot of Mont-Blanc ! Chalet Whymper has been entirely renovated in 2017 into a chic and contemporary style Chalet.

Situated in the heart of Chamonix, the chalet offers 10 bedrooms with en-suite bathrooms and can host up to 22 guests.

With its own private sauna and different communal living spaces, the chalet allows for social gatherings as well as moments for relaxation.

Address and Contact Information:

76 Impasse de L'Androsace, 74400, Chamonix France

iii. Hostels:

Chamonix provides budget-friendly accommodation options for backpackers and solo travelers in the form of hostels. Hostels often feature shared dormitory-style rooms, communal spaces, and kitchen facilities. They offer a social atmosphere, making them ideal for meeting fellow travelers. The Chamonix Lodge and the Vert Hotel are examples of hostels that provide affordable lodging without compromising on the alpine experience.

Best Hostels in Chamonix:

i. **Vert Lodge Chamonix:**

Le Vert Hotel is a hip and affordable boutique-style hotel offering great value accommodation which is hard to find in such a popular ski town.

It is owned and operated by Mountain Lovers and it's located a short walk from the centre of Chamonix.

Experience the very best activities the Alps can offer with outstanding restaurant and bar, premium equipment hire service and knowledgeable staff to help you get the best out of your stay in Chamonix. The management is happy to offer advice on any activity and can create packages to suit all levels of experience from those looking to explore the beautiful local trails, by foot or bike, to paragliding from the various peaks of the valley or even summit attempts of the magnificent Mont-Blanc.

Check in time: 16:00 to 20:00

Check out time: 11:00

Address and Contact Information:

964 Route des Gaillands, Chamonix.

ii. RockyPop Hotel:

The RockyPop Hotel is a new 3 star establishment in the picturesque village of Les Houches, only a 4 minute drive from Chamonix. Its 148 bedrooms allow you to enjoy all that Chamonix has to offer, at affordable prices.

With its innovative concept the RockyPop creates a completely new staying experience, inviting you to enjoy the moment and share good times, whether it is with your partner, your family or your friends. The RockyPop has been designed around simple values all the while having your well-being in mind, with a varied breakfast, a restaurant in food court style, a cocktail bar, live music events, a ski shop, arcade games and plenty of other surprises. The RockyPop has thought of it all! Its Rocky Shuttles are all set to bring you to the ski slopes of Chamonix in the mornings, as well as return you back to the hotel after your day of skiing in the afternoons.

Check-in time starts at 3 pm

Check-out time is 12 pm

Address and Contact Information:

1476 avenue des Alpages, Les Houches, Chamonix

iv. Self-Catered Apartments:

Self-catered apartments are a popular choice for those who prefer more independence and flexibility. These apartments come equipped with kitchen facilities, allowing guests to prepare their meals. They are suitable for families or groups looking for a home-like atmosphere.

Accommodations like La Ginabelle and La Savoyarde Apartments offer a range of self-catered options.

La Ginabelle

La Savoyarde

v. **Mountain Refuges (Refuges de Montagne):**

For adventurous souls seeking an authentic alpine experience, mountain refuges provide shelter high in the mountains. These basic accommodations are strategically located along popular hiking and trekking routes, offering a place to rest, eat, and connect with fellow outdoor enthusiasts.

The Refuge du Plan de l'Aiguille and Refuge du Lac Blanc are examples of mountain refuges in the Chamonix area.

Refuge du Plan de l'Aiguille

Refuge du Lac Blanc

vi. Bed and Breakfasts (Chambres d'Hôtes):

Chamonix offers charming bed and breakfast options that provide a more personalized experience. Hosted by locals, these accommodations often include a hearty breakfast and insights into the region's hidden gems.

La Chaumière Mountain Lodge and Les Tissourds Bed & Breakfast are examples of establishments that offer the warmth of a home away from home.

La Chaumière Mountain Lodge

Les Tissourds Bed & Breakfast

vii. Budget Hotels:

Travelers on a budget can find comfortable and affordable hotel options in Chamonix. These establishments may offer simpler amenities but still provide a convenient base for exploring the town and its surroundings.

Budget-friendly hotels such as Hôtel de l'Arve and Hôtel Le Chamonix are well-located and cater to cost-conscious travelers.

Hôtel de l'Arve

Hôtel Le Chamonix

viii. Luxury Resorts:

For those seeking the epitome of luxury, Chamonix features high-end resorts that provide unparalleled comfort and services. These resorts often include spa facilities, gourmet dining options, and stunning mountain views.

Best Luxury Resorts in Chamonix:

i. **Hôtel Hameau Albert 1er:**

Set on landscaped grounds along the D1506 road, this posh hotel dating from 1903 is 13 km from the peak of Mont Blanc, 9 minutes' walk from the resort center and a 16-minute walk from the nearest ski lift.

Featuring wood paneling and balconies with garden

views, the polished rooms offer flat-screens, DVD players and Wi-Fi access, plus minibars and sitting areas. Upgraded rooms add mountain views and fireplaces. Chalets add designer furnishings and whirlpool tubs.

Parking is free. There's an acclaimed restaurant and a rustic eatery, as well as a sleek bar with live music. A spa offers a steam room, a hot tub, and an indoor/outdoor pool.

Check-in time: 16:00

Check-out time: 12:00

Address & contact information:

38 Rte du Bouchet, 74400 Chamonix-Mont-Blanc, France

+33 4 50 53 05 09

ii. Park Hotel Suisse & Spa:

A 9-minute walk from the Planpraz gondola, this traditional chalet-style hotel is 7.5 km from Mer de Glace, the longest glacier in France. Cozy, rustic rooms have en suite bathrooms and Wi-Fi, plus minibars and flat-screen TVs.

The rooftop spa features panoramic views of Mont

Blanc, as well as a heated outdoor pool, a hot tub, 2 saunas and a steam room. The restaurant has a shaded terrace, and a breakfast buffet is offered. Parking is available. There's also a fitness center.

Check-in time: 15:00

Check-out time: 11:00

Address & contact information:

75 All. du Majestic, 74400 Chamonix-Mont-Blanc, France

+33 4 50 53 07 58

Considerations for Choosing Accommodation:

Location: Consider the proximity of the accommodation to the town center, ski lifts, or hiking trails based on your preferences and planned activities.

Amenities: Assess the amenities offered, such as spa facilities, dining options, and recreational spaces, to ensure they align with your preferences.

Budget: Determine your budget and explore accommodation options that provide value for money without compromising on comfort.

Group Size: The size of your traveling party may influence your choice of accommodation, whether it's a cozy chalet for a family or a shared dormitory for solo travelers.

Seasonal Availability: Chamonix experiences peak seasons for skiing in winter and mountaineering in summer. Ensure your chosen accommodation is available and suits the season of your visit.

Chamonix Mont-Blanc's diverse accommodation options cater to a broad spectrum of travelers, allowing each visitor to tailor their stay to their unique preferences and interests. Whether seeking a luxurious mountain retreat or a budget-friendly hostel, the town provides a welcoming base for exploring the wonders of the French Alps.

Transportation within Chamonix

Navigating the stunning landscapes of Chamonix Mont-Blanc is a seamless experience, thanks to a well-organized transportation system that caters to both locals and visitors. Whether you're looking to explore the town, venture into the surrounding valleys, or access the high-altitude attractions, Chamonix offers a range of transportation options.

1. Chamonix Valley Bus Network:

The Chamonix Valley is well-served by an extensive bus network that connects various neighborhoods, hamlets, and key attractions. The buses operate year-round, providing an efficient and eco-friendly way to explore the town and its surroundings. The bus system is particularly convenient for reaching popular destinations like Les Houches, Argentière, and Vallorcine.

2. Montenvers Train:

The Montenvers Train, also known as the "Mer de Glace Train," offers a scenic journey from Chamonix to the Montenvers-Mer de Glace site. This historic cogwheel train takes passengers through picturesque landscapes, offering breathtaking views of the Aiguille du Midi and the surrounding peaks. At the Montenvers station, visitors can access the Mer de Glace glacier and the Grotte de Glace (Ice Cave).

3. Aiguille du Midi Cable Car:

The Aiguille du Midi Cable Car is an iconic transportation method that takes visitors to one of the highest points in the Mont-Blanc massif. Departing from Chamonix, this cable car ascends to the Aiguille du Midi station at 3,842 meters (12,605 feet), providing unparalleled panoramic views of the Alps. The Aiguille du Midi is a popular starting point for mountaineering and offers access to the Vallée Blanche ski descent.

4. Les Houches and Prarion Gondolas:

Les Houches, a charming village in the Chamonix Valley, is accessible via the Bellevue and Prarion gondolas. These lifts provide access to hiking trails, ski slopes, and scenic viewpoints. The Prarion gondola, in particular, offers stunning views of the Mont-Blanc massif and is a gateway to the Les Houches ski area.

5. **Rental Cars and Taxis:**

While Chamonix is well-connected by public transportation, some visitors may prefer the flexibility of renting a car. Rental car services are available in the town, providing the freedom to explore the surrounding areas at your own pace. Taxis are also accessible for convenient point-to-point transportation.

6. **Walking and Cycling:**

Chamonix is a pedestrian-friendly town, and many attractions and amenities are within walking distance. Strolling through the streets allows visitors to soak in the alpine ambiance and discover hidden gems. Additionally, cycling is a popular mode of transportation, with bike paths and trails crisscrossing the valley for those looking to explore on two wheels.

7. **Shuttle Services:**

During the ski season, shuttle services operate between Chamonix and various ski areas, ensuring convenient access for skiers and snowboarders. These shuttles facilitate transportation to and from popular ski resorts like Brevent-Flegere, Les Grands Montets, and Le Tour.

8. **Electric Buses:**

Chamonix is committed to sustainable transportation, and the town has introduced electric buses to reduce its environmental impact. These eco-friendly buses operate on several routes, providing clean and efficient public transportation.

9. **Electric Scooters and Bicycles:**

Electric scooters and bicycles are available for rent, offering an alternative mode of transportation for short distances. These shared mobility options provide a convenient and environmentally friendly way to explore Chamonix.

10. Transfer Services:

For those arriving or departing from nearby airports such as Geneva, transfer services are available. Shuttle companies and private transfer services offer door-to-door transportation, making the journey to and from Chamonix convenient and comfortable.

Tips for Transportation in Chamonix:

MultiPass: Consider purchasing a MultiPass, which provides unlimited access to the Chamonix Valley bus network, as well as discounts on various lifts and attractions.

Timetables and Schedules: Be mindful of bus and lift timetables, especially during the off-season when operating hours may vary.

Parking: If renting a car, check parking options in advance, as parking spaces in the town center may be limited.

Weather Conditions: Weather conditions in the mountains can impact transportation services. Stay informed about any changes or disruptions, especially during adverse weather.

Chamonix Mont-Blanc's well-organized transportation system ensures that visitors can easily explore the town and its stunning surroundings. Whether ascending to high-altitude peaks, traversing the valleys, or simply strolling through the charming streets, the transportation options in Chamonix provide a seamless and enjoyable experience for all.

Safety Tips for Outdoor Activities

Whether you're hiking, skiing, climbing, or engaging in any outdoor pursuit, following these safety tips will help you enjoy the stunning surroundings while minimizing risks.

1. **Know Your Limits:**

Understand your personal fitness level, experience, and skill set. Chamonix offers activities for all levels, so choose adventures that match your abilities. Avoid pushing yourself beyond your limits, especially in challenging conditions.

2. **Check Weather Conditions:**

Mountain weather can change rapidly. Check weather forecasts and conditions before heading out. Be prepared for sudden shifts in temperature, visibility, and precipitation. Avoid venturing into high-altitude areas during adverse weather.

3. **Inform Others:**

Always inform someone trustworthy about your plans, including your route, expected return time, and emergency contacts. If plans change, update your contacts. This precaution ensures that someone is aware of your whereabouts in case of unforeseen circumstances.

4. **Carry Essential Gear:**

Pack essential gear based on your activity. This may include proper clothing, navigation tools, a first aid kit, a map, a compass, and communication devices like a fully charged phone or a satellite communicator. For winter activities, ensure you have avalanche safety gear.

5. **Dress Appropriately:**

Wear weather-appropriate clothing, including layers that can be added or removed. Use moisture-wicking materials to stay dry, and always have a waterproof outer layer. Proper footwear is crucial, especially for activities like hiking and climbing.

6. **Stay Hydrated and Nourished:**

Bring sufficient water and snacks to stay hydrated and maintain energy levels. Dehydration and fatigue can compromise your decision-making abilities and physical performance, increasing the risk of accidents.

7. **Follow Trail Markings:**

When hiking or trekking, stay on marked trails to avoid getting lost. Pay attention to trail markers and signs. Straying off designated paths can lead to dangerous terrain and potential hazards.

8. **Be Avalanche Aware:**

If engaging in winter sports like skiing or snowboarding, be aware of avalanche risks. Check local avalanche forecasts, carry avalanche safety equipment (transceiver, probe, and shovel), and consider hiring a certified guide if venturing into backcountry areas.

9. Observe Wildlife from a Distance:

Chamonix is home to diverse wildlife. If you encounter animals, maintain a safe distance and avoid disturbing them. Respect wildlife habitats and follow local guidelines for wildlife observation.

10. Respect Environmental Regulations:

Adhere to Leave No Trace principles by minimizing your impact on the environment. Respect wildlife, pack out all trash, and follow any regulations in place to preserve the natural beauty of the area.

11. Be Cautious with Water Activities:

If participating in water activities like rafting or kayaking, wear appropriate safety gear, including a life jacket. Be aware of river conditions, water levels, and potential hazards. Only participate in water activities within your skill level.

12. **Know Emergency Procedures:**

Familiarize yourself with emergency procedures specific to your activity. Understand how to use your equipment, and know the location of emergency services, rescue stations, and medical facilities.

For the fire brigade, call 18

For the police, call 17

For an ambulance, call 15

For mountain Rescue, call +33 (0) 4 50 53 16 89

For vehicle breakdown services, call+33 (0) 6 37 12 81 19 or +33 (0) 7 87 30 31 84

For Chamonix Tourist Office, call+33 (0) 4 50 53 00 24

13. **Stay Informed about Trail Closures:**

Check for any trail closures, maintenance, or restrictions before heading out. Stay updated on local regulations and advisories to ensure a smooth and safe outdoor experience.

14. Learn Basic First Aid:

Having basic first aid knowledge is essential. Learn how to address common injuries, such as sprains, cuts, and hypothermia. Carry a compact first aid kit and know how to use its contents.

15. Hire a Local Guide:

Consider hiring a certified local guide, especially for challenging activities or unfamiliar terrain. Guides possess valuable knowledge about the area, conditions, and safety measures, enhancing your overall experience.

By prioritizing safety and adhering to these tips, you can fully enjoy the outdoor wonders of Chamonix Mont-Blanc while minimizing risks. Whether exploring the trails, hitting the slopes, or summiting peaks, responsible and informed choices contribute to a safer and more enjoyable adventure in this alpine paradise.

Budgeting and Currency Exchange

Planning a trip to Chamonix Mont-Blanc involves careful budgeting and considerations for currency exchange, ensuring a smooth and stress-free experience. From accommodation and transportation to meals and activities, here's a detailed guide on budgeting and managing currency exchange for your visit to this stunning alpine destination.

1. **Research Currency and Exchange Rates:**

Chamonix is located in France, and the official currency is the Euro (€).

Before your trip, research the current exchange rates and monitor any fluctuations. Utilize reliable currency conversion tools or apps to help you plan your budget accurately.

2. **Set a Realistic Budget:**

Determine a realistic budget based on your travel preferences, duration of stay, and planned activities. Consider accommodation, transportation, meals, outdoor excursions, and any additional expenses. Factor in both fixed costs and discretionary spending.

3. **Accommodation Costs:**

Accommodation in Chamonix varies, with options ranging from budget-friendly hostels to luxurious resorts and chalets. Research and book accommodations in advance to secure the best rates. If you're on a budget, consider self-catered apartments or bed and breakfast options.

4. **Transportation Expenses:**

Budget for transportation, including flights or train tickets to Geneva (the nearest major airport), local transportation within Chamonix (such as buses or taxis), and any rental car expenses if needed. Planning transportation in advance can help you find the most cost-effective options.

5. **Meals and Dining:**

Chamonix offers a variety of dining options, from fine restaurants to casual eateries. To manage food expenses, consider a mix of dining out and preparing your meals. Explore local markets for fresh produce and ingredients. Set a daily budget for meals and be mindful of dining costs, especially in popular tourist areas.

6. **Outdoor Activities:**

Chamonix is renowned for its outdoor activities, including skiing, hiking, and mountaineering. Research activity costs, equipment rentals, and any guide fees. If you plan on engaging in multiple activities, explore bundled packages or passes that offer discounts.

7. **Currency Exchange Options:**

Before arriving in Chamonix, exchange a small amount of currency for immediate expenses. Currency exchange options include banks, currency exchange offices, and ATMs. While ATMs provide convenience, be aware of potential fees. Compare exchange rates and fees to find the most favorable option.

8. **Credit Cards and Debit Cards:**

Credit cards are widely accepted in Chamonix, especially in hotels, restaurants, and larger establishments. However, it's advisable to carry some cash for smaller businesses and local markets. Inform your bank of your travel dates to avoid any issues with card transactions.

9. **Emergency Fund:**

Include an emergency fund in your budget for unforeseen expenses or emergencies. This fund can be useful for medical needs, unexpected transportation changes, or any other unplanned situations.

10. **Take Advantage of Discounts and Passes:**

Chamonix offers various passes and discount cards for activities and transportation. For example, the Chamonix MultiPass provides access to the local bus network and discounts on lifts. Research and purchase passes that align with your planned activities to maximize savings.

11. Plan for Tips and Gratuity:

In France, service charges are typically included in restaurant bills. However, it's customary to leave small change as a tip, rounding up the bill. Consider tipping guides, drivers, and service staff based on your satisfaction with the service.

12. Monitor Expenses During Your Trip:

Keep track of your expenses during your stay in Chamonix. Use mobile apps or keep a travel diary to record expenditures. Regularly check your bank statements to monitor card transactions and ensure there are no unauthorized charges.

13. VAT Refunds:

If you make significant purchases, especially in high-end stores, inquire about the VAT refund process. Non-European Union residents may be eligible for a refund on Value Added Tax (VAT) for certain goods.

14. Travel Insurance:

Consider purchasing travel insurance that covers medical emergencies, trip cancellations, and other unforeseen events. Travel insurance provides financial protection and peace of mind during your trip.

15. Plan for Local Events and Festivals:

Chamonix hosts various events and festivals throughout the year. Check the event calendar and plan accordingly. Some events may have admission fees or additional costs.

By carefully budgeting and managing currency exchange, you can make the most of your visit to Chamonix Mont-Blanc while staying within your financial comfort zone. Plan ahead, stay informed about costs, and make informed decisions to ensure a memorable and financially responsible travel experience in this stunning alpine destination.

Sustainable Travel Practices in Chamonix

Travelers to Chamonix can contribute to the region's sustainability efforts by adopting eco-friendly practices and supporting initiatives that prioritize environmental conservation and responsible tourism. Here's a comprehensive guide to sustainable travel practices in Chamonix:

1. **Responsible Accommodation Choices:**

- Choose eco-friendly accommodations that implement sustainable practices, such as energy conservation, waste reduction, and water-saving initiatives.
- Opt for hotels and lodgings certified by recognized sustainability programs or those actively involved in environmental stewardship.

2. **Transportation with Minimal Environmental Impact:**

- Utilize public transportation, such as the Chamonix Valley bus network and electric buses, to reduce carbon emissions.
- Consider walking or cycling for short distances within the town to minimize the environmental impact of transportation.
- If renting a car, choose fuel-efficient or electric vehicles, and carpool when possible.

3. **Leave No Trace:**

- Follow the principles of Leave No Trace by respecting natural environments, staying on marked trails, and properly disposing of waste.
- Carry a reusable water bottle, refill it at designated water stations, and minimize single-use plastics during your stay.

4. **Support Local and Sustainable Businesses:**

- Choose restaurants and shops that prioritize local, seasonal, and sustainably sourced products.
- Support businesses that are part of the "Mont-Blanc Excellence" label, which promotes local products and artisans committed to quality and sustainability.

5. **Respect Wildlife and Nature:**

- Observe wildlife from a safe distance, refrain from feeding animals, and avoid disrupting their habitats.

- Stay on marked trails during outdoor activities to prevent soil erosion and protect fragile ecosystems.

6. **Responsible Winter Sports Practices:**

- When skiing or snowboarding, adhere to designated trails and off-piste regulations to avoid disturbing wildlife and preserve the mountain environment.
- Choose eco-friendly ski resorts that implement sustainable practices in snowmaking, waste management, and energy conservation.

7. **Participate in Sustainable Outdoor Activities:**

- Engage in low-impact outdoor activities such as hiking, trail running, or rock climbing while respecting natural surroundings.
- Hire certified guides who follow ethical and sustainable practices during outdoor excursions.

8. **Contribute to Conservation Initiatives:**

- Participate in local conservation efforts, such as trail maintenance programs or clean-up events organized by environmental organizations in Chamonix.

- Contribute to funds or initiatives that support the preservation of the Mont-Blanc massif and its biodiversity.

9. **Water and Energy Conservation:**

- Conserve water by taking shorter showers, reusing towels, and reporting any water leaks in accommodations.
- Turn off lights, heating, and electronic devices when not in use to minimize energy consumption.

10. **Learn about Local Cultures and Traditions:**

- Respect and learn about the local cultures and traditions of Chamonix, promoting cultural sensitivity and appreciation.
- Choose guided tours or experiences that provide insights into the history, customs, and heritage of the region.

11. **Educate Yourself and Others:**

- Stay informed about Chamonix's environmental challenges and conservation initiatives.
- Share your knowledge with fellow travelers, encouraging responsible behavior and sustainable travel practices.

12. **Reduce Your Carbon Footprint:**

- Minimize your carbon footprint by offsetting your travel emissions through reputable carbon offset programs.
- Choose direct flights when possible and consider alternative transportation options, such as trains, to reduce environmental impact.

13. **Respect Local Regulations and Guidelines:**

- Adhere to local regulations, especially in protected areas and natural reserves, to ensure the preservation of the environment.
- Familiarize yourself with guidelines for outdoor activities, including hiking, climbing, and skiing, to minimize negative impacts.

14. **Attend Sustainable Events and Festivals:**

- Participate in eco-friendly events and festivals that promote sustainability and environmental awareness.
- Support initiatives that showcase responsible tourism practices and encourage community involvement.

15. **Stay in Sustainable Accommodations:**

- Choose accommodations that have obtained eco-certifications, such as Green Key or EarthCheck, indicating their commitment to sustainable practices.
- Support lodgings that prioritize energy efficiency, waste reduction, and community engagement.

By adopting these sustainable travel practices in Chamonix Mont-Blanc, visitors can contribute to the conservation of the region's natural beauty, support local communities, and ensure that future generations can continue to enjoy the pristine landscapes of this alpine paradise.

TRAVEL PLANNER

DESTINATION:

DATES:

MON	TUES	WED	THURS	FRI	SAT	SUN

SIGHTS TO SEE:

PLACES TO EAT:

EXCURSIONS:

FLIGHT DETAILS:

PAMELA COUTLER

TRAVEL PLANNER

TRAVEL PLANNER

DESTINATION:

DATES:

MON	TUES	WED	THURS	FRI	SAT	SUN

SIGHTS TO SEE:

PLACES TO EAT:

EXCURSIONS:

FLIGHT DETAILS:

PAMELA COUTLER

CONCLUSION

A journey through Chamonix Mont-Blanc, as detailed in this travel guide, promises an unforgettable adventure steeped in natural splendor and cultural richness. From the majestic Mont-Blanc massif to the charming town center, every facet of this alpine destination offers a tapestry of experiences.

Navigating through the historical significance, geographical wonders, and vibrant local life, travelers are guided to explore responsibly, respecting the environment and embracing sustainable practices.

Whether indulging in winter sports, discovering local cuisine, or engaging in outdoor pursuits, Chamonix beckons with a harmonious blend of exhilaration and tranquility.

The guide encapsulates the essence of this mountain haven, serving as a companion for those seeking not only breathtaking landscapes but also a deeper connection with the community and an appreciation for the delicate balance between adventure and preservation.

Chamonix Mont-Blanc, with its timeless allure, invites travelers to embark on a journey where nature's grandeur meets cultural charm.

TRAVEL PLANNER

TRAVEL PLANNER

DESTINATION:

DATES:

MON	TUES	WED	THURS	FRI	SAT	SUN

SIGHTS TO SEE:

PLACES TO EAT:

EXCURSIONS:

FLIGHT DETAILS:

PAMELA COUTLER

TRAVEL PLANNER

TRAVEL PLANNER

DESTINATION:

DATES:

MON	TUES	WED	THURS	FRI	SAT	SUN

SIGHTS TO SEE:

PLACES TO EAT:

EXCURSIONS:

FLIGHT DETAILS:

PAMELA COUTLER

Printed in Great Britain
by Amazon

36460908R00106